Magnolia Plantation and Gardens

Magnolia Plantation and Gardens

DEREK FELL

Principal photography by Derek Fell

GIBBS SMITH
TO ENRICH AND INSPIRE HUMANKIND
Salt Lake City | Charleston | Santa Fe | Santa Barbara

First Edition
21 20 19 18   10 9 8

Published by
Gibbs Smith
P.O. Box 667
Layton, Utah 84041

Orders: 1.800.835.4993
www.gibbs-smith.com

Designed and produced by Linda Herman
Printed and bound in China
Gibbs Smith books are printed on either recycled, 100%
post-consumer waste, or FSC-certified papers.

Library of Congress Cataloging-in-Publication Data

Fell, Derek.
  Magnolia Plantation and Gardens / principal photography
by Derek Fell.— 1st ed.
    p. cm.
  ISBN-13: 978-1-4236-0547-8
  ISBN-10: 1-4236-0547-0
  1. Gardens—South Carolina—Charleston. 2. Plantations—
South Carolina—Charleston. 3. Magnolia Gardens
(Charleston, S.C.) 4. Magnolia Plantation (Charleston, S.C.)
I. Title.
  SB466.U7M343 2009
  712'.609757915—dc22
                        2008029493

Contents

Facing: This is Big Cypress Lake in early-morning light. The bald cypress trees—festooned with silvery gray garlands of Spanish moss—grow in shallow water. Strong brace roots help bald cypress trees resist damage from hurricanes.

Left: Here is the Plantation House in early-morning mist, framed by a leaning live oak tree. The house is the third on the site, erected in 1865 and now open to the public as a museum. The property has been home to descendants of the Drayton family for more than 325 years.

Preceding overleaf: The majestic live oak avenue at the entrance to Magnolia Plantation stretches strong, cantilevered branches over an adjacent meadow. The mighty limbs of these venerable oaks transport visitors back in time to an era of American history made famous by the book and movie Gone with the Wind.

Introduction

Facing: *These are daffodils naturalized in a grassy clearing among ancient live oaks known as the Cathedral Grove. Each year Magnolia Plantation is planted with thousands of spring-flowering bulbs to bloom with the azaleas.*

Left: *A maiden statue overlooking a rice pond beside the Ashley River clutches a japonica camellia blossom gathered from Magnolia Plantation's extensive camellia collection that includes both fall-blooming sasanquas and winter-blooming japonicas.*

We are honored to be the twelfth and thirteenth generations of Drayton descendants responsible for the welfare of Magnolia Plantation and Gardens. In addition, there are ten members of a fourteenth generation waiting to continue the family tradition. We all cherish our family heritage and find it remarkable that Magnolia Plantation and Gardens has survived in private family ownership through three and a quarter centuries despite ravages wrought by the American Revolution, the Civil War, damage from the Great Charleston Earthquake of 1886 and, most recently, a direct hit from Hurricane Hugo in 1989.

We hope this book serves as a reminder of a pleasant visit to this exquisite corner of the world, and that you will return to experience Magnolia Plantation through all its seasons.

Twelfth Generation
J. Drayton Hastie Jr.
Nona Hastie Valiunas

Thirteenth Generation
J. Drayton Hastie III
Winslow W. Hastie
Taylor Drayton Nelson
Fernanda Moore Bashaw
Dylan Nelson

History

COPYRIGHT, 1907, BY
DETROIT PUBLISHING CO.

11539   STEAMER LANDING, MAGNOLIA-ON-THE-ASHLEY, CHARLESTON, S.C.

"*Brilliant with azaleas, or magnolias, it centers around a pool of dreamy water, overhung by tall trunks wanly festooned with the gray Florida moss. Beyond anything I have ever seen, it is other-worldly . . . It's perfect. This is the most beautiful spot in the world.*"

—John Galsworthy, *Century Magazine*

Each morning, an orange glow in the eastern sky invariably lights up the horizon beyond Magnolia Plantation and across the wide marsh-fringed Ashley River. The heavy outstretched limbs of ancient live oaks are silhouetted black; wisps of Spanish moss drape from the branch tips to create a ghostly atmosphere, while colonies of leathery resurrection ferns grow out from the deeply fissured bark, taking nourishment from the atmosphere. Tall cypress trees with massive buttressed trunks are reflected in the mirror-smooth lake water, alligators drift like floating logs towards unsuspecting turtles, and the plaintive cry of a peacock pierces the stillness to announce the dawn of a new day. The scene seems prehistoric—as the Carolina Lowcountry

must have appeared when dinosaurs walked the earth.

Confirming Galsworthy's claim that Magnolia Plantation is the most beautiful spot in the world is the 1900 edition of the *Baedeker Guide to America*, a tourist handbook, listing only three sites as their top ranking: Niagara Falls, the Grand Canyon, and Magnolia Plantation. When Magnolia's first residents, Thomas Drayton and his wife, established the plantation for growing rice, the surrounding area was Indian-controlled wilderness, and few would have thought that such a swampy region could possibly result in one of the world's most celebrated homes and beautiful gardens. Fortunately, the property has been cherished as a home by fourteen generations of the Drayton family. Opening its gates to public visitation in 1872, the gardens have long been South Carolina's most popular tourist destination.

A live oak tree overhangs a wide path that leads from the Plantation House to the banks of the Ashley River. Blue ground cover in the foreground is a perennial blue bugle. A plaque explains that the remains of J. Drayton Hastie Sr. are interred inside the tree.

A high-elevation view of Magnolia's Biblical Garden, containing plants mentioned in the Bible. The garden honors the memory of three garden superintendents. This image was published in Time magazine in a story about biblical gardens.

Arrival of the Drayton Family

It was in 1671 that Thomas Drayton, son of a Barbados plantation owner, immigrated aboard the sailing ship *Mary* to the new territory of Charles Town in the British colony of Carolina. There he met his future wife, Ann Fox, and received as a wedding gift from her father an estate of two thousand acres along the banks of the Ashley River. They built one of the first substantial plantation houses of the Carolina Colony twelve miles from the present port of Charleston. The newlyweds tried to grow silkworms, olives, and citrus fruits before finding rice a more profitable crop. To establish a sense of order in the midst of this wilderness, they made a formal garden behind the house, called Flowerdale. Over the years this small parterre garden—the oldest continuously cultivated flower garden in North America—expanded to encompass more than five acres of cypress swamp.

The roots of the Drayton family are said to extend as far back as the Norman Conquest of England, when

Aubrey de Vere (later Great Chamberlain to Henry I) landed with William the Conqueror and, for distinguished service at the Battle of Hastings, was awarded land near Northampton to build a fortified manor known as Drayton House. Since the Norman Conquest, Drayton House has been the residence of descendants of Aubrey de Vere.

In the early thirteenth century, Sir Walter de Vere dropped the family name "de Vere" and assumed the Saxon name of his domain, "Drayton." Over the past nine hundred years the Drayton family has spread far and wide. One branch settled in Barbados, but concerned about overpopulation, Thomas Drayton and his son, Thomas Jr., left Barbados to resettle in Charleston.

The original plantation house was destroyed by fire in the 1790s. Though no illustration of the original house survives, John Drayton, Governor of South Carolina and founder of the University of South Carolina, described it as a beautiful country seat, "A Mansion House of brick . . . in some respects not dissimilar from the center part of Drayton House, Northamptonshire, England." A second house was burned in 1865 by

General Sherman's renegade Union troops at the end of the Civil War. Forced to seek safety in the Blue Ridge Mountains at the end of the war, when Sherman was marching to Columbia, Reverend John Drayton returned to find the plantation house a blackened shell. However, the gardens were flowering so profusely beyond the house that they inspired him to rebuild. Also, he later opened the property to the public and charged an admission to help pay his debts, creating what has become one of North America's oldest man-made tourist attractions.

Since the roads out of Charleston were unpaved and usually rutted in Colonial times, the Ashley River was the preferred means of travel to and from Magnolia Plantation, and so boatloads of visitors journeyed by paddle steamer to see what plantation life was like. The garden's fame spread throughout North America and to Europe, attracting famous artists, writers, and statesmen, who took home reports of a garden beyond comparison with anything at home or abroad.

The most significant expansion to the gardens occurred during the ownership of the Reverend John

The porch along the west side of the Plantation House has a view out into the garden and to a sea of color from flowering trees and shrubs. The hanging basket features a vining nasturtium.

Drayton in the 1840s. A pastor at the local St. Andrews church, he developed tuberculosis and decided to spend time outdoors and "work the soil" on the advice of his doctor. Further expansion occurred after his health improved and he married Julia Ewing of Philadelphia. In order to woo her affections for moving to the South, he imported from Philadelphia plants she liked. These included the beautiful camellias grown there in conservatories. His intention was to make the gardens as romantic as possible, "to create an earthly paradise in which my dear Julia may forever forget Philadelphia and her desire to return there." He was aided in his ambition by a new philosophy of garden design that had emerged in England. Rebelling against the formality of French and Italian gardens, landscape designers in England sought a more natural garden environment, one that could produce a more romantic atmosphere. The Reverend Drayton realized that this new romantic style was well suited to Magnolia Plantation and would please Julia. Although many American gardens followed this English style of romanticism, Magnolia is believed to be the oldest-surviving example.

To achieve the new English style of picturesque naturalism, he created a series of trails that meander around lakes with water reflections as clear as a mirror. He was the first to use Indica hybrid azaleas for ornamental effect, finding perfect growing conditions in the sandy soil, lightly shaded by massive live oaks and bald cypress trees. A tender member of the rhododendron family developed in Belgium, these rebloom each spring in company with blue wisteria, white dogwoods, and masses of flowering bulbs to create a glorious spectacle of color.

Until the 1840s, even camellias were relatively unknown in the Carolinas. They were introduced to England from Asia, and the first American import arrived in 1798. Camellias became popular as conservatory plants among wealthy homeowners in Philadelphia, but it was the Reverend Drayton who realized how well they could perform outdoors in Lowcountry woodlands, given the acidic soil and mild winters. By the 1850s, Magnolia's camellia collection was the most extensive in North America. Sasanqua varieties bloom magnificently in November and December, followed by japonicas in January, February, and March.

A principal endeavor at Magnolia Plantation is to maintain color through four seasons and to make the experience of a visit to Magnolia a pleasure for all the family. In summer, crepe myrtles, mophead hydrangeas, and southern magnolias (for which Magnolia Plantation is named) reach flowering peak; in fall, Magnolia glows with cannas, caladiums, and the russet colors of deciduous trees. Year round, the Conservatory tropical garden features hundreds of exotic plants under glass, including bananas, palms, and bromeliads—an appropriate tribute to Magnolia's ties to the beautiful Caribbean island of Barbados.

The Nature Center and Petting Zoo are popular with children of all ages; also thrilling for children are the Nature Train rides and Audubon Swamp Garden, where water birds and alligators can be observed from the safety of boardwalks and elevated observation decks.

The American Revolution

After considerable harassment by American patriot Frances Marion, "The Swamp Fox," the British occupied Magnolia Plantation and were able to draw a fatal siege line across the Charleston Peninsula in the spring of 1780. This forced the surrender of Charleston in spite of its larger force of Continental troops. Three years later, the British commander Lord Cornwallis allowed himself to be trapped on the Yorktown peninsula, ending the American War of Independence.

Antebellum Life

Until emancipation in 1865, Magnolia was a slave plantation, with a population of approximately forty to forty-five blacks at the start of the Civil War. A street of slave cabins survives on the grounds, and these have been restored in order to interpret African American life at Magnolia from the antebellum period through the twentieth century. The Reverend Drayton, owner during the last twenty-nine years of that era, affectionately referred to his slaves as his "black roses," and in addition to spiritual work among them, he built a school for the education of children of slaves, in violation of state law. The Reverend Drayton's two aunts, Angelina and Sarah Grimke, agitated for the abolition of slavery and for women's rights. A speech they gave in Philadelphia's Pennsylvania Hall, advocating an end to slavery, sparked mob violence.

Right: This high-elevation view of School-house Pond and its rustic red bridge is seen through the branches of a flowering pear. The pond is named for a nearby schoolhouse. Now an administration office, the school-house was built to educate the children of slaves, in violation of state law.

Facing: The Bamboo Garden offers exquisite reflections, especially from the crest of an arched Oriental-style footbridge that crosses a narrow inlet. Swamp lichen on the bald cypress trunks colors the bark pink.

Today, the Biblical Garden, situated south of the Plantation House, is dedicated to the memories of four black supervisors: Adam Bennett (1838—1910), John Bennett (1878—1926), Ezekiel Bennett (1886—1949), and Willie Fay Leach (1904—1986).

The American Civil War

The American Civil War began on January 10, 1861, when a ninety-man infantry from the South Carolina Military Academy fired on the U.S. Government steamer *Star of the West*, and prevented its reinforcement of Fort Sumter. They were cadets from the Military Academy, now known as The Citadel. Most prominent families in the South had relatives in the North, and the conflict tore the nation apart. Sons of Colonel William Drayton of Philadelphia even took opposite sides. Brigadier General Thomas Fenwick Drayton took the Confederate side and opposed his brother, Admiral Percival Drayton of the Union Navy, during the invasion of Hilton Head. Though defeated by his brother, Brigadier Drayton survived the war to end his days as the president of a railroad, while Admiral

Drayton continued to make a successful career in the navy.

The Reverend Drayton owned property in Flat Rock, North Carolina, a Charleston summer enclave since the 1840s, which served as a refuge for the Drayton family during General Sherman's advance towards Atlanta. It was here, at Ravenswood, that he received news from freed plantation slave Adam Bennett of the burning of his plantation house by Union troops. Bennett had walked 250 miles to bring news of the destruction and the willingness of former plantation slaves to help rebuild.

The Reverend Drayton was forced to sell a sea island plantation and portions of Magnolia to recover from the Civil War. To his dismay, he also had to consent to the strip mining of phosphate over what he retained, and evidence of this remains today. An eighteenth-century summerhouse he owned at nearby Summerville was dismantled and moved by barge downriver to Magnolia, where it was mounted on the burned-out ground-floor walls of the plantation house.

A slave cabin is located in a grove of trees beside the petting zoo. The interiors have been preserved in the same living condition as pre—Civil War days. In a separate location, an entire street of slave cabins has been restored to create a museum.

The Great Earthquake

At 9:50 p.m. on August 31, 1886, the earth around Magnolia Plantation shook violently. Walls of the Plantation House were severely damaged, and a large crack appeared in the family tomb. The city of Charleston was damaged by the largest earthquake to hit the southeastern United States within living memory. Many downtown buildings were reduced to rubble and makeshift tents had to be erected to house the displaced. The Plantation House was restored, and it continued to serve as a home to successive families of Draytons until 1976, when owners J. Drayton

Hastie Sr. and his wife, Fernanda, moved into the plantation manager's residence, allowing the main house to be opened to the public as a museum. A well-stocked gift shop occupies the ground floor. The upper floors and bedrooms are now a gallery featuring mostly wildlife paintings and antiques from the Reverend Drayton's town house or his Summerville house.

Expansion of the Gardens

After emancipation, rice cultivation at Magnolia was no longer economical. It demanded a great deal of labor cultivating the seedlings, transplanting them

into shallow lakes, and harvesting the grains of rice. At harvest time, workers were also needed to scare away flocks of ricebirds (also known as bobolinks) that could destroy a third of the crop during their migration south. The opening of the gardens to the public allowed many of the freed slaves to remain on the plantation as paid workers.

The abandoned rice ponds were dredged deeper to deter aquatic weeds, and a labyrinth of footpaths was created around them. The Reverend continued to add azaleas and camellias along the walkways for a floral extravaganza like the South had never seen. Yellow

Lady Banks roses, white Cherokee roses, blue wisteria, and other spring-flowering vines extended color into the topmost branches of the trees.

In 1889, at age seventy-four, the Reverend Drayton found himself with no son to inherit the plantation, and so he willed the property to his daughter, Julia, who married William S. Hastie of Charleston. Since the death of the Reverend, the stewardship and maintenance of the gardens has been carried on by direct descendants of Julia.

In the late 1920s, C. Norwood Hastie, then owner of Magnolia, considered a reconstruction of the original

Camellia trees create a tunnel with their lofty branches inside Magnolia's camellia garden. The camellia was first grown as a conservatory plant until the Reverend Drayton discovered it could be grown outdoors without protection at Magnolia Plantation. The most famous member of the camellia family is the tea plant, still cultivated in South Carolina.

Plantation House. He even had architectural plans drawn up and purchased a prerevolutionary brick house in Charleston to provide authentic construction materials. However, the stock market crash of 1929 and subsequent Depression thwarted this endeavor, and so the bricks were used as edging for many of Magnolia's garden walkways.

Although the Reverend Drayton was responsible for the greatest influence on the gardens, and first opened the gardens to the public as a means of recovering financially from the Civil War, it was J. Drayton Hastie Sr. who steered the gardens through several more recent crises. In 1975, he bought out his brother's interest and resigned as president of Reeves Telecom Corporation to devote full time to the management of Magnolia, determined to increase attendance and make the gardens self-sufficient. "That decision came within an ace of breaking me," he said. After Hastie had used his personal finances to stimulate tourism and make needed improvements, the Arab oil embargo of 1976 cut attendance to a tenth of what was needed to break even. Worried that he might have to sell the property, he persevered through the economic downturn and introduced several innovative attractions. These included a petting zoo, wildlife observation tower, a nature train, and several horticultural features including a replica of an eighteenth-century holly maze, a sixteenth-century herb garden, a biblical garden, a tropical Conservatory, a bamboo garden, and Audubon Swamp Garden; also, he opened the main house for tours and renovated facilities for weddings and special events.

Hurricane Hugo

When Hurricane Hugo made landfall in September 1989, Magnolia took a direct hit. The damage from high winds and torrential rain was so extensive, massive live oak trees and cypress trees toppled across the lakes, and Mr. Hastie thought he might not be able to re-open. At great personal expense, he hired a helicopter to clear away the debris so that the gardens would not be further damaged by heavy equipment.

In keeping with Magnolia's policy of wildlife conservation, more than five hundred acres are now preserved as a wildlife sanctuary. Nature trails for hikers, joggers, and cyclists wind through woodlands, swamps, and across dikes that border the Ashley River. These remote areas are also accessible by the Nature Train, which leaves from the parking area, and by canoe rental from the jetty at the bottom of a wide path known as the Broad Walk. The wildlife tower is within a short walk from the garden, allowing expansive views of the historic tidal rice fields and of bald eagles that frequently nest and hunt along the river. A feature of the biking and walking trail is a large Indian burial mound. Most of the artifacts found here were removed to the Smithsonian Institution or displayed at the Plantation House.

The plantings at Magnolia are continually changing. Bulbs for naturalizing—such as daffodils and grape hyacinths—are ordered in lots of ten thousand to make big, bold splashes of color. The collections of azaleas, camellias, and hydrangeas are not only being added to but also grouped to create a mass of color and ready identification during their blooming times.

Spring

"I have seen gardens, many gardens, in England, France, in Italy. I have seen what can be done in great hot-houses, and on great terraces, what can be done under a roof, and what can be done in the open air with the aid of architecture and sculpture, and ornamental land and water, but no horticulture that I have seen devised by mortal man approaches the unearthly enchantment of the azaleas at Magnolia."

—Owen Wister,
Lady Baltimore magazine

Magnolia Plantation is in zone 8 on the USDA's plant hardiness map. Frosts are infrequent and snow may fall once in ten years. Spring flowering occurs at Magnolia Plantation in early March, when warm spells energize sleeping buds into bloom. First to flower are masses of daffodils that have naturalized along the woodland trails. Saucer magnolias flaunt their large pink blossoms high into the tree canopy,

Facing: The Schoolhouse Pond is rimmed with azaleas, their colors exquisitely reflected in the mirror-like surface of the water. This highly reflective quality is caused by tannin from bald cypress roots staining the water dark.

Left: Southern Indica azaleas, first introduced to America at Magnolia Plantation from Europe, produce a symphony of color.

quickly followed by a riot of other early-flowering trees, such as ornamental peach, cherry, and almond. A parade of colorful flowering bulbs follow the daffodils. Tulips crowd the parterre beds of Flowerdale; Dutch iris (*Iris hollandica*) bloom through the lawns fronting the Ashley River, and colonies of red and pink amaryllis glare from the shade of the majestic live oaks. French anemones in all shades of red and blue mingle their satinlike flowers with thousands of shimmering trumpet-shaped white flowers of indigenous atamasco lilies.

Almost every morning in spring, a mist from the river pervades the garden, creating ghostly silhouettes, muted colors, and a supernatural aura. After the sun burns through the mist, the garden is a tapestry of sunlight and shadows. Flower beds

Right: The high-arched Oriental bridge that crosses the Bamboo Pond is a favorite subject of artists and photographers. Steps are cut into the lower ends of the arch to allow easy access to the top, and a hole at the peak allows a young bald cypress tree to grow through the bridge.

Facing: A white Victorian-style gazebo provides shelter from rain beside the Bamboo Pond. A path surrounds the pond, directing one's attention to its beautiful water reflections.

are at their brightest and foliage sparkles in the clear sunlight. In the late afternoon, the garden is often bathed in reddish tones. Sunsets can be stunning, painting the sky and water shades of red, orange, and apricot.

Right: The street of slave cabins is framed by the branches of a massive live oak tree. The cabins were occupied by descendants of slaves until the 1980s.

Facing: Wisteria vines coil up into the leaf canopy beside Big Cypress Lake. Wisteria is native to China and Japan and has seeded itself throughout the garden, some of the vines extending to the tops of the loftiest loblolly pines that grow to ninety feet tall.

The Glory of the Azaleas

Peak flowering of azaleas occurs in March and April. They overlap their exotic floral display with the last camellia japonicas and the peak flowering of blue wisteria that takes floral color high into the sky. Many of the hybrid Indica azaleas grow to twenty-five feet high in all shades of red, from pale pink to deepest crimson, from lilac blue to deep purple, plus white. Adding to this exotic display is a collection of native American azaleas collected from southern states to create a native azalea garden. These include the yellow-and-pink-flame azalea (*Rhododendron austrinum*) and the bright pink pinxter azalea (R. *prunifolium*).

Facing: The Long Bridge identifies the garden at Magnolia Plantation more than any other structure. Considered French in style because of its sleek lines and trellised handrails, it was designed by the Reverend John Drayton when he decided to expand the gardens and make them more romantic to please his wife.

Left: Spent azalea petals color a path red beside Big Cypress Lake. Accumulations of Spanish moss, seen draped from the branches of a crepe myrtle tree in the background, vary from one year to the next, their abundance believed to be an indicator of quality air circulation.

Two early-flowering climbing roses—both from China—can grow to forty feet and higher, flowering with the azaleas and arching their canes out over the lakes. These are the yellow double, thornless, cluster-flowered Lady Banks rose (*Rosa banksiae*) and the single white, exceedingly thorny Cherokee rose (*R. laevigata*).

Birds in the thousands arrive to mate and nest in spring, including flocks of white egrets, herons, and anhingas that nest in the Audubon Swamp Garden. At the Nature Center and Petting Zoo, peacocks are active courting peahens by fanning their iridescent green-and-blue feathers. Magnolia even has a family of rare white peacocks, their tail feathers resembling an explosion of snowflakes when spread apart. Similarly, the tom turkeys fan out their black-and-tan tail feathers to attract a mate, and call with a musical gobbling sound.

Alligators become more active as temperatures increase, sunning themselves on special wooden ramps built over the rice ponds and along the grassy dikes. The largest is Bubba, a fourteen-foot male weighing more than a thousand pounds. He likes to sun himself on an island in the Audubon Swamp Garden, visible from the boardwalk. Females hollow out a depression on high ground to lay their eggs and cover it with leafy material.

Here, water reflection in spring is viewed from the Long Bridge across Big Cypress Lake. To create such a tranquil environment, the Reverend John Grimke Drayton dredged the former rice pond deeper. Fresh water from the nearby Ashley River, controlled by a sluice gate, maintains a steady water level throughout the year.

The Gardens of Historic Charleston

The port city of Charleston is little changed from Colonial times, when rich merchants built grand mansion houses and gardens along the harbor known as the Battery. The interest among early settlers in ornamental gardens, and the area's large number of indigenous plants (such as massive live oaks, tall swamp cypress, and palmettos), drew European horticulturists, including Englishman Mark Catesby (1679—1749), who published a beautiful illustrated work entitled *The Natural History of Carolina, Florida and the Bahama Islands*. Its two hundred colored plates are similar in quality and accuracy to Audubon's famous portfolio of North American birds.

Facing: Several gazebos are placed at strategic intervals throughout the garden, mostly as rain shelters. They also add ornamentation and face a beautiful view. This structure beside the Ashley River is surrounded by indigenous young sabal palms. Mature sabals sprout long, arching greenish-yellow flower clusters that bear thousands of blue-black fruits the size of a small olive.

Left: An Oriental-style footbridge spans an inlet of the Ashley River, leading to a wildlife tower and nature trails. A live oak tree spreads its sinuous branches over the span.

Summer

"A painter of flowers and trees, I specialize in gardens and freely assert that none in the world is as beautiful as this. It consigns the Boboli of Florence, the Cinnamon Gardens of Colombo, Conception at Malaga, Versailles, Hampton Court, the Generalife at Granada, and La Mortola to the category of 'also ran.'"
—John Galsworthy, Century Magazine

Magnolia Plantation remains a flowering paradise throughout summer, with the peak flowering of pink and blue mophead hydrangeas and crepe myrtles in mostly shades of red and pink, plus white.

Spanish moss is an epiphytic plant that persists year-round, drawing its nourishment from the atmosphere. A type of bromeliad known botanically as *Tillandsia usneoides*, it is related to the pineapple plant. Specimens can grow long, pendant strands of modified gray leaves that twist and twine like an old man's beard, up to four

Facing: A white heron hunts for frogs in the shallows of Big Cypress Lake.
Left: This Bird Girl statue by Sylvia Shaw Judson is a replica of a bronze original that once stood in the Bonaventure Cemetery.

feet in length. The tiny green flowers are fragrant but inconspicuous and appear in summer. Spanish moss is most prolific on live oak trees since they have wide outstretched branches from which the Spanish moss can cling. It also hangs from the branches of pines, cypresses, Southern magnolias, and crepe myrtles.

Ever-blooming roses such as 'Carefree Beauty' and 'Flower Carpet' produce a strong flush of color in early summer, when nights remain cool, and flowering continues intermittently into fall.

Any discussion of rose growing in South Carolina would be incomplete without acknowledgement of the work of a Charleston nurseryman, John Champneys, who in

Right: Rose 'Carefree Beauty' is massed in a bed in front of the Plantation House. Other roses used in the garden are the shrub rose 'Flower Carpet' and the climbing roses 'Lady Banks' (yellow) and 'Cherokee' (white).

Facing: This fine example of a horticultural maze is a replica of the holly maze at Hampton Court Palace in England. Although holly is used in the Magnolia maze, it includes some camellia bushes for added ornamental interest. An elevated platform allows adults to steer children through the maze to the middle.

1811 crossed *Rosa chinensis* 'Old Blush' with R. *moschata*, a white single-flowered musk rose. This resulted in 'Champney's Pink Cluster', the first rose to be hybridized in America. The vigorous plant displays semi-double, fragrant, pale pink roses up to two inches across, in dense clusters.

Champney's gave cuttings to a neighbor, Phillip Noisette, an immigrant French botanist and nurseryman, who recognized its commercial value at a time when plant patents were not available, and sent cuttings to his brother, Louis, a nurseryman in Paris. As a result, by 1820, 'Champney's Pink Cluster' was grown throughout France and other countries of Europe under the name "Noisette." Louis used Champney's rose as a

Right: This crepe myrtle hedge along the main driveway is backed by a pair of mature southern magnolias. Native to India, crepe myrtles relish the warm summers and mild winters of Magnolia Plantation.

Facing: A rare white peacock fans its tail feathers to attract a mate. Both white and multicolored peacocks have free range at Magnolia Plantation, and they are a popular attraction of the petting zoo. Their wings are not clipped, and it is a spectacular sight to see them in flight, trailing their long tail feathers.

parent in further crosses, creating a whole family of Noisette roses. In Redoubté's famous portfolio of rose paintings, *Les Roses* (its publication sponsored by Empress Josephine), 'Champneys Pink Cluster' is identified as R. *noisettiana*.

A hike or leisurely bike ride around the rice ponds at Magnolia is often rewarded by the sight of egret or heron hatchlings being fed or learning to fly. Canoeing on the rice ponds may even reveal newly hatched alligators sunning themselves on driftwood and sometimes even on the backs of resting turtles, which later will become a favorite food.

Days are generally warm and sunny, with intermittent thunderstorms bringing tropical downpours. Several gazebos surrounding Big Cypress Lake provide shelter from these sudden rainstorms.

Many of the lakes bloom with water lilies and lotus. Clumps of pampas grass produce silky white flower plumes that will persist into winter, and daylilies in myriad colors bloom into fall. Tropical hibiscus and bougainvillea, which survive winter under cover, bloom nonstop into fall.

Shrubby oleanders in shades of red and pink are mostly grown in tubs. Gardenias fill the garden with fragrance in lightly shaded areas. Although native to China, the gardenia was named for Dr. Alexander Garden, a Charleston physician, by Carl Linnaeus, the Swedish botanist.

This massive live oak tree was toppled during a storm. Normally live oaks can withstand hurricane-force winds, but often a torrential rain loosens the soil so that the tree's anchorage is undermined.

John Bartram (1699—1770), the noted American botanist who lived in Philadelphia, collected indigenous North American plant species under the auspices of King George III, and one of his greatest introductions to Europe is the Southern magnolia (*Magnolia grandiflora*) for which Magnolia Plantation is named. Since the garden at one time had a double row of these handsome broadleaf evergreen trees leading from the main entrance all the way to the Ashley River, Bartram's specimens may have come from Magnolia Plantation. In early summer, the trees produce large, fragrant white flowers up to ten inches across, resembling doves in flight.

Magnolia also features a large number of indigenous palmettos. These produce fanlike fronds and, in summer, showers of greenish-white flowers, followed by black berries.

Colonies of cannas, with erect paddle-shaped leaves, flaunt orange gladioluslike flowers in front of the plantation house and around the lakes. Also, the hardy bananalike *Ensete musa* will survive winter outdoors. Two other exotic foliage plants that maintain

Donkeys graze a meadow that is part of Magnolia's petting zoo. They share the meadow with a herd of Shetland ponies. Goats, foxes, and deer are also popular attractions of the petting zoo in addition to birds such as turkeys and geese. Flocks of wild turkeys are often seen along the nature trails.

vibrant color during summer are caladiums, with large heart-shaped leaves, and lace-leaf coleus, both of which like shade. Caladiums are native to South America, and they often display three distinct colors in their leaf pattern, such as red, pink, and green. One variety, 'Candidum', even has white leaves with pronounced red veins. Magnolia's collection of coleus—maintained by taking cuttings of the best colors—includes varieties with orange, red, and yellow leaves, highlighted with chocolate markings.

Magnolia's Bridges

Because the garden is designed around a series of former rice ponds, Magnolia has a number of distinctive bridges, the most famous of which is the Long Bridge, which crosses a corner of Big Cypress Lake close to the Plantation House. More than 160 years old, and built by the Reverend Drayton, it has a sleek design with trellised handrails and three arches. The whiteness of the bridge is in stark contrast to the shadowy overhanging live oak branches and the dark, still water. It is a favorite motif of artists who visit the garden. Photographs of the bridge

have appeared in many books, magazines, calendars, greeting cards, newspaper articles, and even jigsaw puzzles. It is one of the most recognizable garden structures in the world, a trademark of the garden, and a symbol of the South.

A similar white bridge, with handrails in a crisscross design, provides access to a small island at the far end of the same lake. A more rustic bridge, painted Chinese red, crosses Schoolhouse Pond, named for the proximity of the schoolhouse for plantation slaves that today serves as an administration office. A white Japanese-style moon bridge with a high arch crosses a corner of the Bamboo Pond and provides a high-elevation view of the surrounding area, including several mature bald cypress coated with an unusual pink lichen. A Chinese-style bridge, with a white chinoiserie pattern of slats for the rails, has a slightly lower arch and a longer span. It crosses an inlet of the Ashley River at the far end of Big Cypress Lake.

Autumn

"Dawn emerges. Ancient oaks are silhouettes, ethereal and ghostly, arms outstretched, heavy with the weight of Spanish moss. Water is a black mirror whose calm is shattered when an alligator lunges for an unsuspecting coot in the Audubon Swamp. Nature's awakening on the Ashley River near Charleston, South Carolina, remains primordial despite its civilized overlay of Magnolia Plantation along its banks for the past three hundred years."

—Tom Woodham,
Southern Accents magazine

Autumn is one of the most pleasant times of year at Magnolia Plantation. When cool temperatures return to the garden, the change in leaf colors can be dramatic, and visitors in November will invariably encounter a remarkable transformation of the swamp cypresses. Unlike the

Left: A clump of perennial gaillardia, a native American wildflower, blooms among parterre hedges in the herb garden, located in front of the Plantation House.

Facing: Here is an overall view of the Audubon Swamp Garden in fall, with the spire-shaped bald cypress trees changing color to orange. A deciduous conifer, the bald cypress drops its leaves as winter approaches and sprouts new bright-green needles in spring.

Right: The boardwalk through the Audubon Swamp Garden allows visitors safe close-up views of wildlife, including otters and alligators, plus many kinds of aquatic birds, including egrets, herons, and anhingas.

Facing: These drifts of native swamp sunflowers are seen through the trunks of bald cypress in the Audubon Swamp Garden. Swamp sunflowers bloom even with their roots submerged in shallow water.

loblolly pines that are evergreen, the cypresses have deciduous needles that drop after changing from green to orange. Swamp maples, liquidambars, and sedge grasses also turn russet shades.

The Southern live oak (*Quercus virginiana*) is the most conspicuous deciduous tree at Magnolia Plantation, and also the most majestic. Though its leaves are small and slender like a willow and its acorns are small, it is semi-evergreen, dropping most of its leaves during autumn months. It then erupts with a new flush of bright green leaves in spring. The sparseness

of leaves on the branches in winter produces a wonderful silhouette on many of the mature trees, some of which are three hundred years old, up to eighty feet high, and one hundred feet wide.

The Audubon Swamp Garden

Composed of sixty acres of tupelo and cypress swamp, a walk through the Audubon Swamp Garden is a good way to complete a visit to Magnolia Plantation, so the contrast between the cultivated garden and the Low-country wilderness from which it sprang can be

Facing: Camellia sasanqua 'Sparkling Burgundy' blooms at the entrance to the Bamboo Garden. Magnolia's collection of camellias is the most extensive in the United States. The blossoms are so numerous that, from a distance, they are often mistaken for rose bushes.

Left: Camellia sasanqua 'Bonanza' blooms near the Long Bridge, seen in the background. Sasanqua camellias have a more spreading habit than japonicas and bloom mostly in fall, followed by the taller japonicas in winter and early spring.

realized. Home to scores of wildlife, including alligators, otters, egrets, herons, anhingas, and turtles, its name honors the great North American artist John J. Audubon, who stayed at Magnolia Plantation as a guest of the Reverend Drayton and obtained waterfowl specimens for his portfolio of bird paintings.

The Swamp Garden's eerie beauty is best appreciated by strolling along a series of raised dikes and a wide, winding boardwalk, with observation decks to safely view and photograph many of the swamp's creatures. Indigenous atamasco lilies bloom on hummocks in spring,

water lilies float their beautiful fragrant blossoms in summer, and masses of swamp sunflowers (*Bidens aristosa*) colonize vast stretches of shallow water in fall. It is an enchanting place to visit through all the seasons.

Migrating monarch butterflies are plentiful in fall, and Magnolia's lakes are a vital stopover for birds migrating south.

One of the last flowering trees to bloom is the Franklinia tree (*Franklinia alatamaha*), first discovered growing wild near Savannah in 1765 by John Bartram (1699—1777) and his son William. Confined to a

Right: Spanish moss, a type of bromeliad related to the pineapple, is not a parasite, and it lives off nutrients in the atmosphere. This colony is backlit by early-morning light in the Audubon Swamp Garden. Herons and egrets often line their nests with it.

Facing: A sunrise streaks long shadows from bald cypress trees across the surface of the Audubon Swamp Garden.

small area of sand dunes along the Altamaha River near Savannah, it was last seen in the wild in 1803. Since the tree is highly susceptible to poor drainage and root rot, it is believed that the planting of cotton introduced a disease organism that killed off the wild stands, so that today the only surviving trees are those in cultivation. The pure-white saucer-shaped flowers appear in late summer and early fall on a small deciduous tree that resembles a camellia. The flowers have a golden crown of anthers and are fragrant. In fall, the leaves often turn orange and red. The Franklinia tree

has long, sinuous multiple trunks that are especially beautiful when pruned of lower branches to reveal its shining charcoal-gray-colored bark.

Of all the fall-flowering woody plants, nothing can compete with the camellia sasanquas. Bushy in habit, they cover themselves in mostly red, pink, and white flowers, resembling a rose bush from a distance. Native to China and Japan, camellia sasanquas are a broadleaf evergreen tree with a mature height of about ten feet. It is much more compact and slightly smaller flowered than its winter-flowering cousin, the japonica.

Caladiums are a tender South American member of the aroid family (which includes jack-in-the-pulpits). They are used extensively throughout the garden for their colorful heart-shaped leaves and heat tolerance. After frost kills the tops, the bulbs are lifted and over-wintered indoors.

A border of coleus (foreground) shows its spectacular leaf colors. Native to Java, these tender perennials are killed by frost; but cuttings are taken of the most beautiful colors and propagated indoors over winter for replanting the following spring. This path leads to the Conservatory.

Also flowering in fall are varieties of cassias, especially the popcorn cassia (*Cassia didymobotrya*), displaying spires of spherical flowers that resemble clusters of popcorn. Conspicuous along the main drives and throughout the swamp garden are the berry displays of yaupon holly (*Ilex vomitoria*), heavenly bamboo (*Nandina domestica*), and firethorn (*Pyracantha coccinea*). Heavenly bamboo is not a bamboo but a twiggy shrub growing to ten feet high, with a bamboo appearance, and massive clusters of bright red berries throughout winter. Yaupon holly is indigenous to the site. It reaches a mature height of fifteen feet, the weeping evergreen branches loaded with bright red berries that persist well into winter. Firethorn can grow to twenty feet, bending its red-berry-laden branches to the ground.

Flocks of wild turkeys are often seen along the hiking and biking trails, busily gorging themselves with fallen berries and acorns from the live oak trees.

Winter

"Animals and birds are an integral part of the scene, from peacocks found nesting in the 18th century herb garden to the great wild egrets and herons flying from tree to tree among the marshland."

—*Christian Science Monitor* magazine

Charleston area gardens such as Magnolia were mostly designed as "winter gardens"—a season that extended from November through April—for summers were too hot for comfortable living. Charlestonians generally sought relief from summer's heat by moving inland to summer homes in the Blue Ridge Mountains.

Magnolia Plantation enjoys mild winters, tailor made for growing camellias that relish sharp winters but not frost, and warm summers. Introduced from Asia by way of Europe, the japonica camellias are

Left: A yellow-flowering popcorn shrub is in company with a sabal palm beside Big Cypress Lake. A type of cassia from Asia, it blooms until fall frost. The common name is derived from the clustered flower buds that resemble popcorn.

Facing: This live oak at Magnolia Plantation, on the banks of the Ashley River, seems to have near-human characteristics. The gnarled thick trunk, the spreading snakelike branches, and the ghostly effect caused by mist produces an eerie supernatural aura.

59

now a symbol of the South, extensively used in floral arrangements during the Christmas holiday season in company with branches of berry-bearing holly and pyracantha.

Magnolia's Camellia Collection

Camellias were first planted at Magnolia Plantation in the 1840s. Though well known as a conservatory plant, they require no protection to flower spectacularly outdoors at Magnolia. The Japanese camellia (*Camellia japonica*) blooms from January to April in mostly white and shades of pink and red. The slightly smaller-flowered sasanqua camellia (*C. sasanqua*) blooms from October through December in a similar color range. A third group, the reticulatas, flowers with the japonicas and includes the largest flowers of all

Facing: A display of C. japonica *varieties, showing their wide color range, is arranged on a bench beside the Bamboo Pond. Many are heirloom varieties saved from extinction and collected from all over the southern states. For this initiative, Magnolia Plantation received a Heroes of Horticulture award.*

Left: C. japonica *'Lady Clare' is an heirloom variety first imported to England from Japan in 1877. Also known as 'Akashigata', it was renamed by the British for commercial sales in the western world.*

camellias, including 'Captain Rawes', which displays pink blooms up to seven inches across.

The Magnolia collection has grown to several thousand plants, representing more than nine hundred varieties. At least fifteen varieties planted prior to World War I survive in the collection, including several specimens from the 1840s era. Some have trunks over fifteen inches in diameter and forty-eight inches in circumference.

Almost 150 registered camellia varieties originated at Magnolia, either as natural hybrids discovered in the garden or crosses made in the nursery. Plans are underway for the addition of several new camellia gardens, including one devoted to antique varieties, another featuring all-white varieties, and a reticulata garden.

Right: Native loblolly pines tower above all else in the garden, seen here at dusk along the Ashley River. Growing up to ninety feet high, they produce soft, long needles and large cones, and are an important lumber tree in southern states.

Facing: Bald cypress trees in the Audubon Swamp Garden produce beautiful silhouettes in early-morning light even in winter. The buttressed trunks and the sparse number of side branches help the trees resist hurricanes and give them a prehistoric appearance.

Right: Once used as a freshwater reservoir for Magnolia Plantation's inland rice fields, and reverted to swamp, the sixty-acre Audubon Swamp Garden provides a sanctuary for wildlife and some of the best fishing within the property.

Facing: Entrance to the Conservatory features a Camellia sasanqua. Further along the path is a sago palm, a member of a family of ancient plants known as cycads. The cycads predate palms in the evolutionary chain and once provided food for dinosaurs. Charleston is the northern limit of its hardiness.

Magnolia honors the camellia with two festivals each year. One in October salutes *Camellia sasanqua* while the other in January recognizes the peak flowering of *C. japonica*, culminating with the Coastal Carolina Camellia Show, held the fourth week in January.

In 2007, Magnolia Plantation received a "Heroes of Horticulture" award from the Cultural Landscape Foundation for the restoration of its camellia collection.

The Washington, D.C., foundation presents the award each year to significant landscapes in danger of being lost. To further protect the camellia, Magnolia Plantation and Gardens initiated the Great Gardens of America Preservation Alliance, a consortium of public gardens in Southern states, aimed at preserving antique camellias and azaleas in danger of being lost to cultivation.

Right: A statue of Father Neptune greets visitors to the Conservatory, an unheated area where specimens of tropical plants are a reminder of Magnolia Plantation's ties to the Caribbean island, where the Drayton family once farmed sugarcane.

Facing: A meandering path lined with teak benches takes visitors through the Conservatory into a junglelike atmosphere, where exotic plants such as bromeliads, heliconias, and orchids thrive in the frost-free sanctuary.

Magnolia's Conservatory

In recognition of the Drayton family's Barbados connection, a Conservatory near the garden entrance houses a collection of tropical plants popular in Barbados gardens. Although the structure is beautiful year-round, winter is an especially good time to visit, for that is when potted poinsettias create a dramatic display among plantings of dragon palms, crotons, heliconias, and other exotic trees and shrubs.

Inside and outside the Conservatory are several beautiful specimens of Japanese sago palm, or cycad (*Cycas revoluta*), a member of an ancient family of plants that predate the dinosaurs. Charleston is the northern limit of its hardiness.

Joel Poinsett (1779—1851), a native of Charleston and first ambassador to Mexico, introduced the poinsettia (*Euphorbia pulcherrima*) to Charleston from Mexico, in addition to other exotic Central American species. Today, the poinsettia is as much a symbol of the Christmas holiday season as holly and mistletoe.

Right: A poinsettia display in the Conservatory during winter honors Joel Poinsett (1779—1851), first U.S. ambassador to Mexico. Born in Charleston, in 1882 he sent to several Charleston nurseries plants of the poinsettia he discovered in Mexico. Today, poinsettias are the most popular gift plant at Christmas.

Facing: Here, the Plantation House is framed by the branches of an ancient live oak. This is the view that greets visitors when they drive in from the Charleston road.

Conclusion

Facing: This simple bench at the entrance to Flowerdale is balanced between two live oak trees. As the trees added girth, they completely engulfed the ends of the seat, creating a good place to sit and admire the secluded parterre garden.

Left: This is an incredibly vibrant spring display viewed from the porch of the Plantation House. The long canes and yellow flower clusters of a Lady Banks rose extend high into the tree canopy. Red azaleas, white bridal wreath, and pink peach blossoms add to the floral extravaganza.

"Nowhere else on earth are the azaleas and camellias more spectacular than here; and nowhere else is the setting so magical. The source of the magic is easy to trace, for Magnolia is a garden in a swamp that produces its haunting spell."

—Henry Mitchell, *Connoisseur* magazine

Given its ephemeral quality, the survival of a garden like Magnolia over a period of 325 years is remarkable. Yet year after year, in all seasons, garden historians, garden writers, garden designers, painters, and other visitors continue to visit Magnolia Plantation to experience its unique beauty.

Although many visit only to experience the garden, which is never the same from one season to the next or even one spring to the next, the area around Charleston abounds with other attractions. Not to be missed is the historic section of downtown Charleston with its beautiful architecture, and Fort Sumter out in the harbor, where the first shots were fired at the start of the Civil War. Many smaller city gardens are open to the public during the Spring Festival of Houses and Gardens that runs from mid-March to mid-April. Also, other historic plantations such as Boone Hall (used for the filming of *Gone with the Wind*), Middleton Place, Drayton Hall, and Cypress Gardens are available to tour.

Sabal palm, also known as cabbage palmetto, bears rounded heads of fan-shaped leaves splayed out like a windmill. Here, a lone tree is silhouetted against a sunset along the Ashley River.

About the Author

Derek Fell made his first visit to Magnolia Plantation in 1979 to interview the late J. Drayton Hastie for an article entitled "Great Gardens of America" for Woman's Day magazine. This began a series of annual visits at the invitation of Drayton Hastie Sr. to photograph the gardens for publicity. As a consequence, Fell authored articles for Connoisseur, Americana, Pace, New Choices, Hemispheres, Southern Accents, and Nouveau magazines, winning awards for Best Magazine Article twice from the Garden Writers Association.

The Carolina Lowcountry

The Carolina Lowcountry is a nature-lover's paradise, especially the coastal plain that extends from Charleston south to Beaufort and on to Savannah, Georgia. A distance of one hundred miles as the crow flies, its shoreline extends along estuaries, bays, and countless islands. Beaufort is a historic small port town with a shorefront of southern mansions built by wealthy merchants during Colonial times, the town's wide streets arched over by magnificent live oak trees. Close by are boat ramps that provide access to one of North America's largest tidal wildlife sanctuaries—the ACE Basin, a nature preserve that covers 134,710 acres of wilderness. Meandering creeks and slow-moving placid rivers are home to alligators, bald eagles, egrets, and wood storks. These tranquil waterways lead to tidal salt marshes and palmetto-fringed beaches, and they also provide a glimpse of the immense rice culture that once made the area prosperous. The ACE Basin encompasses three main rivers—the Ashepoo, the Combahee, and the Edisto—the first initial of each river contributing to the name ACE. Experienced guides and kayaks can be rented to explore this unspoiled sanctuary.